Teac otes
for Gu ding

The Emperor's New Clothes

Teacher's notes by Alison Kelly
Roehampton University
and Suzanne Maile
Sheen Mount School

Contents

Essential information

National Curriculum level: 2A

Genre: traditional

Word count: 1,321

High frequency words

a/an	about	all	am	and	are	as
at	away	back	be	been	but	called
can	can't	come	could	day	did	do
don't	door	down	for	from	go	going
had	have	he	help	here	his	if
in	is	it	just	laugh	like	look
love	make	me	more	much	must	new
no	not	of	off	on	once	one
out	people	play	push	put	said	see
so	take	that	the	their	them	they
this	time	to	two	up	us	very
want	we	went	what	who	will	with
would	yes	you	your			

Interest words and phrases

loom	desperate	absolutely	fabulous
splendiferous			

Background

Many children will already know Hans Christian Andersen's tale of the emperor whose desire for the finest clothes leaves him vulnerable to the canny rogue dressmakers who persuade him that their invisible outfit is the best in the world. This retelling captures all the humour of the original, and adds new and lively detail. We have Boris, the emperor's hapless dresser, and the irrepressible Slimus and Slick who effect the scam with such success. Better still is the silent presence of the emperor's dog, whose outfits mirror the emperor's and provide a constant undercurrent of detail and humour.

Introducing the story

Before you start the reading session or sessions, spend a little time preparing with your group.

Start the session by producing a selection of either clothes from the role play area or maybe some hats. You might like to include some "royal" costumes and crowns.

Ask the children whether they like dressing up, and what special occasions they have had to dress up for in the past (parties, weddings, shows or plays maybe). Bear in mind that some children are very keen to dress up, others strongly dislike wearing fancy clothes for special occasions. They may appreciate the emperor's foolishness all the more.

Tell them that they are going to read a story about a very vain emperor who LOVED dressing up, and was very proud of his amazing outfits.

Show the children a copy of the book and ask if they know the story already. Explain that it is a traditional story, set "long ago". Remind them of other such stories the class has read recently. Ask them if they think these stories really happened.

Check that they understand what an emperor is, telling them emperors are addressed as 'Your Excellence'. Practise bowing and saying 'Your Excellence' together.

Share learning objectives with your group.

The children are going to learn or practise the following:

- Making inferences about characters
- Using word structure to decode new words.

You might say:

- We are going to see what we can guess about characters in the story from clues in the text and the pictures.
- We are going to practise learning to read new words from what we have already read or what we already know.

Now go on to the Walkthrough (see overleaf).

Walkthrough

The walkthrough allows you to "warm" the text for the children by taking them through it without actually reading it.

- You might use it to identify key vocabulary, language patterns and concepts that children could need support with
- You can identify phoneme-grapheme relationships that are to be practised
- It can be a way to identify key 'thinking points' in the story (e.g. where predictions might be made, characters' thoughts inferred and so on).

Using a copy of the book, look through it with the children. We have suggested pause points and prompts.

Talk through the first chapter with the children, drawing their attention to the emperor's clothes habit.

You could read pages 4 to 5, asking the children what the effect of the ellipses are (to give the idea of time passing).

But the emperor had a problem. The royal procession was in two weeks' time, and he had nothing to wear.

7

Highlight the problem on page 7, drawing their attention to the phrase 'royal procession' as necessary.

Pages 8-9 introduce Boris, who tells the emperor how many outfits he has (7,322).

"You must have something, Your Excellence," said Boris, his servant. "You already have seven thousand, three hundred and twenty-two outfits."

"But I've worn them all before," moaned the emperor.

8

"I want to look so amazing, so fantastic, so *splendiferous*, that people will talk about me for years to come."

"I see," said Boris, looking rather glum. It was Boris who had to take care of all the emperor's clothes.

9

You might ask:

- Is that a lot of outfits?
  You could digress into mathematics – how many more outfits does the emperor have than you, or the children? Can they write the number he has in numerals?
- Read the word 'splendiferous' with the children syllable by syllable.
  Why is this word in italics? How should we read it? All read the emperor's words together with appropriate intonation.
- Why is Boris looking glum? Do you know what "glum" means? Can we all try looking glum?

Go on to page 18, where Slimus and Slick are to be found explaining to the emperor that only the cleverest of people can see their magic clothes. Discuss this with the children.

"We make magical clothes!" said Slimus.

"Magical?" said the emperor, sounding interested.

"Yes," said Slick, with a sly smile. "Our clothes can only be seen by clever people."

18

You might ask:

- Do you think they can really make magic clothes?
- Why are 'Slimus' and 'Slick' such good names?

You could discuss the word associations, and also the alliteration which makes for a particularly effective pairing.

Now turn to page 21.

- Why are Slimus and Slick laughing so hard?

Chapter 3

The two cheats

As soon as they were alone, Slimus and Slick laughed until their bellies ached and their faces turned purple.

21

The children should now be ready to read independently. This can be done over several sessions, depending on their experience and ability. We have allowed for two sessions, but you might take more or fewer.

Independent reading and strategy check

Before the children begin reading, include a strategy check to help them tackle difficult or unfamiliar words. **You might say:**

- Let's remember what we do when we can't read a word.
  Elicit suggestions from the children, e.g. blend the phonemes, read ahead.

Ask the children to read aloud, a little at a time, either all together or in turns, whilst you listen and monitor. Encourage them to use cues to work out unfamiliar words, and praise fluent reading or good use of strategies.

For assessment purposes, you may want to use the chart on pages 30–31 to note strategies that each child uses, or errors or comments that he or she makes, during the reading.

Now ask the children to read chapters 1-3 (i.e. pages 1-27) whilst you monitor and record strategies.

Chapter 1

Nothing to wear

Once upon a time there was an emperor who *loved* clothes. He really didn't care about anything else.

3

He ignored his soldiers...

4

avoided his advisors...

hated plays...

5

...and only liked riding in the park so he could show off his amazing outfits.

But the emperor had a problem. The royal procession was in two weeks' time, and he had nothing to wear.

7

"You must have something, Your Excellence," said Boris, his servant. "You already have seven thousand, three hundred and twenty-two outfits."

"I want to look so amazing, so fantastic, so *splendiferous*, that people will talk about me for years to come."

"But I've worn them all before," moaned the emperor.

8

"I see," said Boris, looking rather glum. It was Boris who had to take care of all the emperor's clothes.

9

"Are you sure this one won't do?" Boris asked hopefully, picking a velvet and gold suit from the pile.

"Boris," said the emperor, in a stern voice.

"Er, yes, sire?" said Boris.

"Who is the emperor here?"

10

"You are, Your Excellence," replied Boris.

"Right. And if I say I want new clothes, then I mean it!"

"Go and find me the finest clothes-makers in town," ordered the emperor. "At once!"

11

"I'm off to have a snooze," the emperor added. "It's been a very tiring morning."

12

Chapter 2

Slimus and Slick

Boris spent all day looking for an incredible outfit. He wasn't having much luck, until...

13

Pause after page 13.

Look at Boris' advertisement for the clothes-makers and the long line of people applying for the job.

- You could role-play Boris asking each applicant why they want the job, and what's so special about their clothes-making.
- At a later date, children could design their own outlandish costumes for the emperor.

Now ask the children to read on to page 18.

...two strangers rushed up to him. "We're the finest clothes-makers in the world," they said. "Take us to the emperor at once."

14

When they arrived at the palace, the strangers pushed past the palace footmen and burst into the emperor's room.

"Who are you?" shouted the emperor, angrily. He was busy choosing his afternoon coat and hated being interrupted.

15

"We are Slimus..."

"and Slick..."

"...at your service," they said, and bowed.

16

The emperor just stared at them.

"Haven't you heard of us?" said Slimus, looking shocked.

"Um, well... no," admitted the emperor. He hated not knowing things.

17

"We make magical clothes!" said Slimus.

"Magical?" said the emperor, sounding interested.

"Yes," said Slick, with a sly smile. "Our clothes can only be seen by clever people."

18

Pause after page 18.

- Slimus and Slick say that their special clothes can only be seen by 'clever' people. What do you think they really mean?

Now ask the children to read on to page 24.

"They will be absolutely invisible to anyone stupid," Slimus explained.

"Anyone who can't do their job properly won't be able to see them either," Slick added.

Boris gulped. "What if I can't see the clothes?" he thought.

19

The emperor was very excited. "Make me a magic suit this minute," he cried.

"It won't be cheap," said Slimus and Slick. "We only use the very best material."

"Take this," said the emperor, handing them a sack of money. "You can work in the palace – take anything you want. Only get to work. I want that suit!"

20

Chapter 3

The two cheats

As soon as they were alone, Slimus and Slick laughed until their bellies ached and their faces turned purple.

21

"The fool believed us!" cried Slimus. "We're going to have lots and lots of *lovely* money."

They set up their looms in the palace and ordered in the finest silks and the most expensive gold thread.

But they didn't use any of it. Instead they sold it all for lots more money.

22

"Is there anything else you need?" asked the emperor.

"Yes," Slick replied. "Five fudge cakes, ten tubs of vanilla ice cream and a constant supply of chocolate. That would really help our work."

"But you mustn't see a thing until it's finished," Slick told the emperor. "We want it to be a fantastic surprise."

Every day the emperor crept past their door, listening to the loom going back and forth. He was desperate to know how the suit was coming along.

24

Pause after page 24.

- Make sure the children understand what a loom is and how it works.
- Give support in decoding 'desperate' and 'fantastic' syllable by syllable if necessary.

Now ask the children to read on to page 27.

"I know," he thought. "I'll send Boris along to find out."
But when Boris went in, he could see nothing but empty looms.

"What do you think of our wonderful work?" asked Slick.
"Such a charming pattern, isn't it?" said Slimus.

25

"Oh crumbs," thought Boris. "I can't see a thing. I must be stupid."

"Well," demanded Slimus. "Have you got nothing to say?"

26

Boris gulped. "It's, er, fantastic," he lied. "Absolutely, um, great. I'll tell the emperor I'm very pleased with it."

He hurried off to tell the emperor how fabulous his new clothes were. Slimus and Slick smiled to themselves, and went back to eating cake.

27

Pause after page 27.

You might say:

- Boris has to go and tell the emperor how special the new clothes are. What do you think Slimus and Slick say to each other after he leaves the room?

Suggested session 2

If you are reading the story in two sessions, you might like to go over the story so far. What do the children remember from the previous session? Look through the first part of the book to refresh their memories.

When you are ready, ask the children to read chapters 4 and 5 (pages 28-47), whilst you monitor and record strategies.

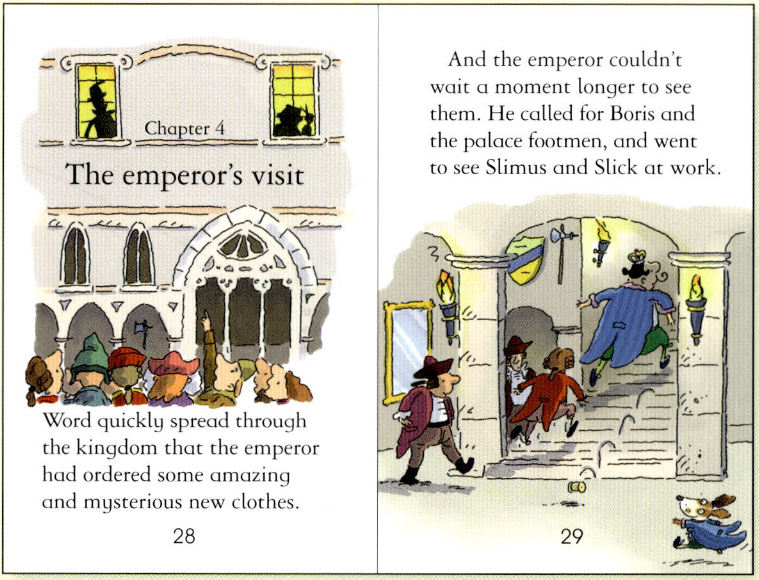

Chapter 4

The emperor's visit

Word quickly spread through the kingdom that the emperor had ordered some amazing and mysterious new clothes.

28

And the emperor couldn't wait a moment longer to see them. He called for Boris and the palace footmen, and went to see Slimus and Slick at work.

29

"Oh Your Excellence," said Slimus, bowing low. "We're so pleased to see you!"

The emperor looked at the loom, then looked again. "This is terrible," he thought. "I can't see anything. I'm not worthy of being emperor!"

30

But aloud he said, "It's magnificent."

"Really very tasteful," added Boris.

The palace footmen were worried. Each thought the other could see the magic material. "Splendid," they said in unison.

31

Slimus and Slick pretended to take the material down from the loom. They made cuts in the air with huge scissors and sewed using needles without any thread.

Everyone clapped loudly. The emperor even gave Slimus and Slick a gold medal each for their excellent sewing.

32

On the morning of the royal procession, the emperor went to put on his new clothes. He was filled with nervous excitement.

33

"Would Your Majesty care to undress?" said Slimus. "Then we'll put on your clothes in front of the mirror."

"I'll bring over the cloak," said Slick. "Boris, pick up the train, will you?"

"This is your shirt, Your Majesty," said Slimus. "See, it's as light as a spider's web."

Slick smiled. "Oh it fits *so* well," he said.

Then the palace footmen bent down, just as if they were picking up a train. The emperor admired himself in the mirror one last time.

"Well, I'm ready," he said. "Don't I look splendid, Boris?"

"Yes, Your Excellence," said Boris, looking straight up at the ceiling.

"Then open the palace doors," said the emperor. "Let the royal procession begin."

Chapter 5

The royal procession

The crowd gasped as the emperor emerged. Everyone had heard that only clever people could see his clothes.

38

"What a wonderful outfit," they cried.

"Such a magnificent pattern," said a woman.

The emperor smiled to himself. "These are my most successful clothes ever," he thought, and added a spring to his step.

"Let me see him," cried a small child, who was stuck at the back of the crowd.

40

The child was lifted up on his father's shoulders, so he could see the emperor in all his glory.

"Ooh!" said the child. "The emperor's got nothing on!"

Everyone around the child fell silent and looked at the emperor again.

41

Pause after page 41.

You could ask:

- Was it a good thing that the little boy told the truth?

Now ask the children to read on to page 47.

"He's right you know," said his father. "The emperor is *naked*!"

Then, faster than a spreading fire, a whisper whizzed through the crowd.

Soon the whole crowd was chanting. "The emperor's got no clothes on!"

The emperor heard their words and shivered. Suddenly, he felt very cold.

43

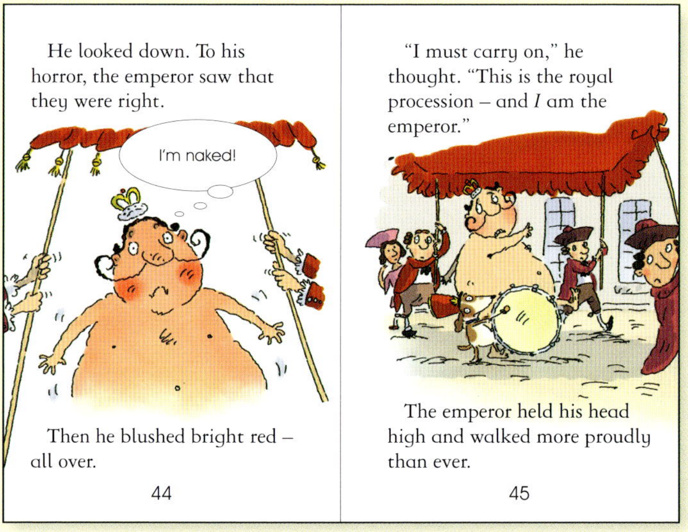

He looked down. To his horror, the emperor saw that they were right.

Then he blushed bright red – all over.

44

"I must carry on," he thought. "This is the royal procession – and *I* am the emperor."

The emperor held his head high and walked more proudly than ever.

45

Meanwhile, Slimus and Slick were packing their bags full of money, getting ready to flee the palace forever.

"We tricked him!" they cried, and cackled with glee.

46

As for the crowds – they were enjoying the best procession ever. Boris, of course, wasn't having such a good day...

"Oh well," he thought, as he followed the emperor home. "At least one thing turned out as he wanted. People *will* talk about the emperor for years to come."

47

At the end of the story, you could ask:

- Who do you think was the cleverest character?
- Remind the children that this is a traditional story. How do we know that? When was it set? How can you tell?

Now return to the text (see overleaf) to discuss whether the children's answers and predictions were correct, and talk about their approaches.

Return to the text

The return to the text allows you to reinforce teaching points, e.g. checking children's understanding, identifying and reinforcing successful decoding strategies.

Look through the story again to recap on strategies the children have used for decoding unfamiliar words (e.g. phonic, graphic, context or syntax).

You might say:

- I really liked the way (***child's name***) worked out how to read (***word or phrase***) – can you tell us how you did it?

Talk about the story as a whole.

You might ask:

- Were there any parts of the story that surprised you?
- Which part (or character or picture) did you like best?
- Did you like the ending? Can you think of a different way the story could have ended?
- Do you know any other stories like this?

Further reading

Young Reading Series One

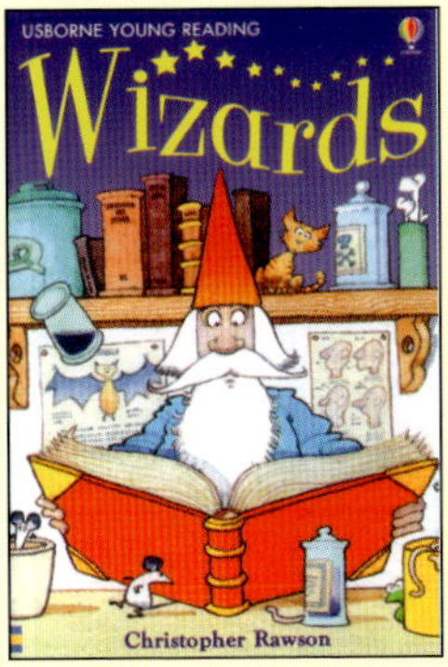

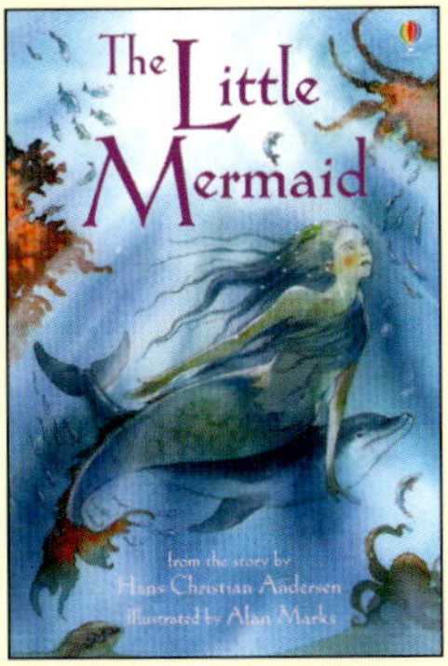

Young Reading Series Two

There are over 100 titles available in the Young Reading series, and more are being added all the time. To find out about all the titles available, go to **www.usborne.com**

Guided Reading Record

Text: *The Emperor's New Clothes – high level 2*

Class:..

Group:..

Date:..

Teacher/
Teaching Assistant:..

At Level 2A, it is expected that children:

1. Extend the range of books read, sharing and comparing reasons for preferences.

2. Infer characters' feelings in fiction and consequences in logical explanations.

3. Use syntax, context and word structure to build a store of vocabulary as they read for meaning.

Name: Comments: Target:	Name: Comments: Target:
Name: Comments: Target:	Name: Comments: Target:
Name: Comments: Target:	Name: Comments: Target:

About the Usborne Reading Programme

The Usborne Reading Programme is a collection of over 150 titles for beginner readers, graded in seven levels from very beginners to fully confident readers. Launched in 2002, it has since sold almost 5 million copies worldwide.

The Usborne Reading Programme combines vivid, engaging writing with captivating full-colour illustration on every page. From classic tales to lively non-fiction, there is something to appeal to everyone.

From one level to the next, there is a clear progression in terms of subject, style, narrative length, sentence structure and vocabulary, giving children the satisfaction of mastering real books and making measurable progress without overstretching them and causing them to lose enthusiasm.

Non-fiction titles at all levels draw on the expertise of a range of specialists in their subject, ensuring that the books are not only engaging but authoritative: for example, Eva Schloss, stepsister of Anne Frank, advised on **Anne Frank**, and John Woolley of the Captain Cook Memorial Museum in Whitby advised on **Captain Cook**.

The Reading Programme advisers

The Reading Programme has been developed in consultation with **Alison Kelly**, a leading expert in the teaching of reading, who helped to draw up the seven-level framework (see pages 36-37). Alison worked for many years as a primary school teacher in London, and is currently a Senior Lecturer in Education at Roehampton University, teaching about all aspects of literacy.

Suzanne Maile is assistant headteacher at Sheen Mount Primary School in south-west London, a thriving school with a reputation for outstanding teaching and learning. Suzanne is responsible for curriculum development and initial teacher training at Sheen Mount, and has extensive experience in teaching guided reading at all levels. She is also a teacher tutor at Roehampton University, and a consultant teacher for Richmond LEA.

Together, Suzanne and Alison have chosen a selection of titles from the Reading Programme that are particularly suitable for guided reading, and produced comprehensive teacher's notes, packed with ideas and guidance for guided reading sessions.
The range of titles in the Reading Programme provides wide scope for further reading at every level.

The Usborne Reading Programme and the National Curriculum

The Usborne Reading Progamme is fully integrated with the National Curriculum for English at Key Stages 1 and 2, encouraging children to develop fluent and accurate reading across a range of texts, subjects and styles.

Selected titles from all levels of the Reading Programme are available as Guided Reading packs, comprising six copies of the book plus comprehensive teacher's notes. Guided Reading packs represent a selection of text types, and are carefully graded within levels 1-4 of the National Curriculum.

Text type: European folktale
NC level: 1C

Text type: Asian folktale
NC level: 1B

Text type: adapted children's classic
NC level: 1A

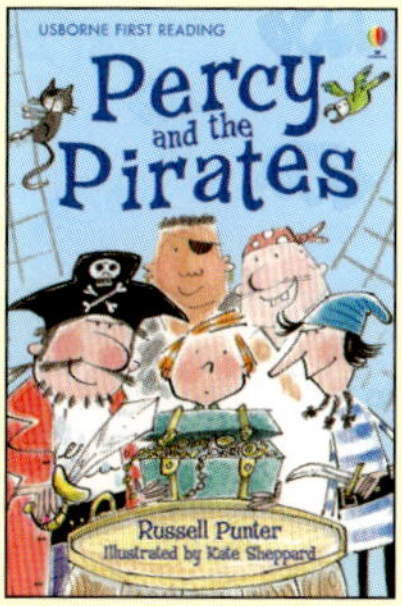

Text type:
original fiction
NC level: 2C

Text type:
original fiction
NC level: 2B

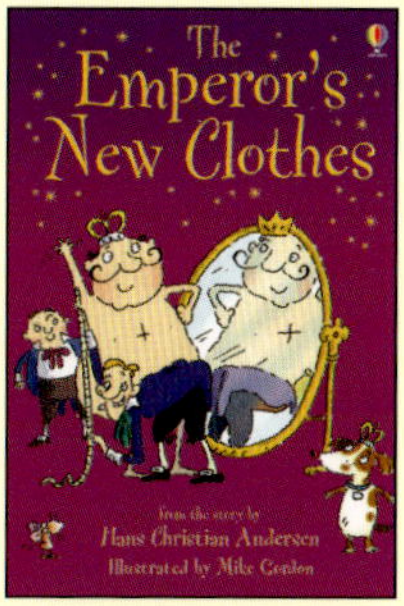

Text type:
classic fairytale
NC level: 2A

Text type:
myths and legends
NC level: 3C

Text type: adapted
children's classic
NC level: 3B

Text type:
adapted classic
NC level: 3A

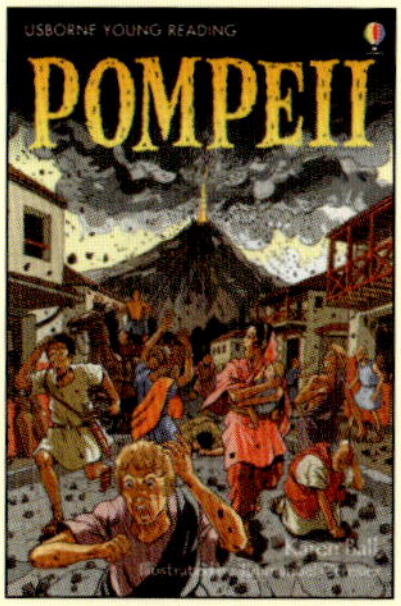

Text type:
non-fiction (history)
NC level: 4C

Text type:
biography
NC level: 4B

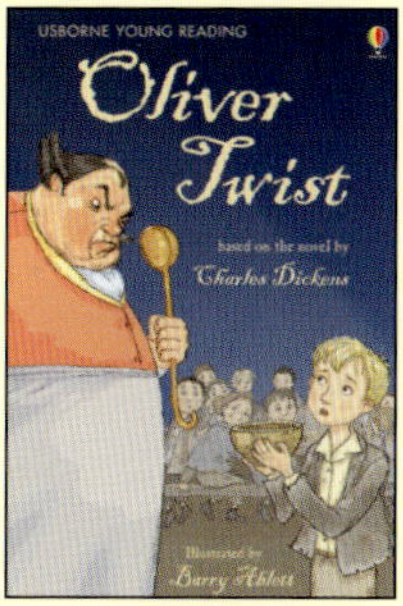

Text type:
adapted classic
NC level: 4A

The Usborne Reading

	Number of words	Themes
First Reading Level One National Curriculum level 1	up to 150	Classic tales (e.g. Aesop's Fables) and folktales
First Reading Level Two National Curriculum level 1	up to 250	As Level One, including less familiar folktales
First Reading Level Three National Curriculum level 1-2	up to 450	As Level Two plus original fiction and non-fiction (natural history life cycles)
First Reading Level Four National Curriculum level 2	up to 750	As Level Three plus classic fairy tales
Young Reading Series One National Curriculum level 2-3	1,000-1,500	Fairy tales, fantasy, fiction, non-fiction ("the story of...")
Young Reading Series Two National Curriculum level 3	2,000-2,500	As Series One plus adapted classics
Young Reading Series Three National Curriculum level 3-4	4,000-5,000	History, biographies, classics

The elements above are intended as guidelines only, and whilst distinctions between different levels remain clear,

Programme framework

Content	Vocabulary
Short single narrative followed by reading and comprehension puzzles	Simple everyday vocabulary, familiar items
Single narrative plus character sheets and/or maps, and puzzles	More descriptive and evocative vocabulary, always clear in context
Single narrative with repeated elements, plus character sheets and/or maps, no puzzles	Powerful verbs and adjectives, clear in context
Single narrative	More exotic elements and controlled use of idiom
Several linked stories or one longer narrative in chapters. Direct and indirect speech, intertextual references	Wide-ranging everyday vocabulary
Single narrative in chapters. Introduce irony and subplot, allow opportunity for inference and deduction	More challenging, building on Series One; specialist or technical terms explained
Single narrative in chapters. Assumes some relevant background knowledge	Building on Series Two, may assume knowledge of specialist or technical terms

exceptions may sometimes be made to individual specifications in the interests of narrative or style.

Notes

This book belongs to ...

....

Tips for Talking and Reading Together

Stories are an enjoyable and reassuring way of introducing children to new experiences.

Before you read the story:

- Talk about the title and the picture on the cover. Ask your child what they think the story might be about.
- Talk about what a vet does. Has your child ever taken a pet to the vet with you?

Read the story with your child. After you have read the story:

- Discuss the Talk About ideas on page 27.
- Talk about the things you find at the vet on pages 28–29 and then find them in the pictures of the story.
- Do the fun activity on page 30.

Have fun!

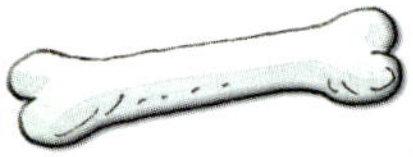

Find the bone hidden in every picture.

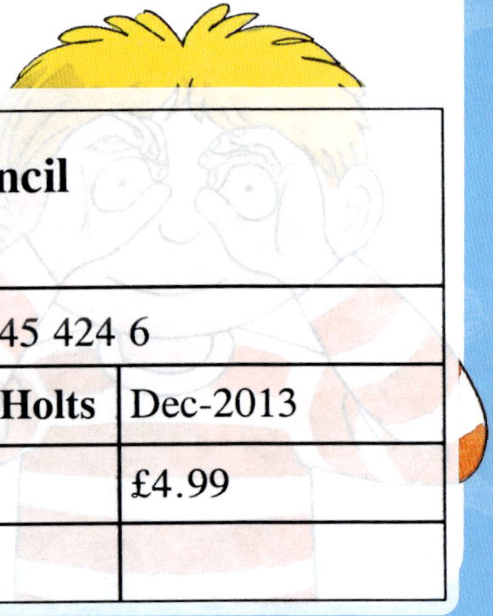

For more hints and tips on helping your child become a successful and enthusiastic reader look at our website www.oxfordowl.co.uk.

Going to the Vet

Written by Roderick Hunt and Annemarie Young
Illustrated by Alex Brychta

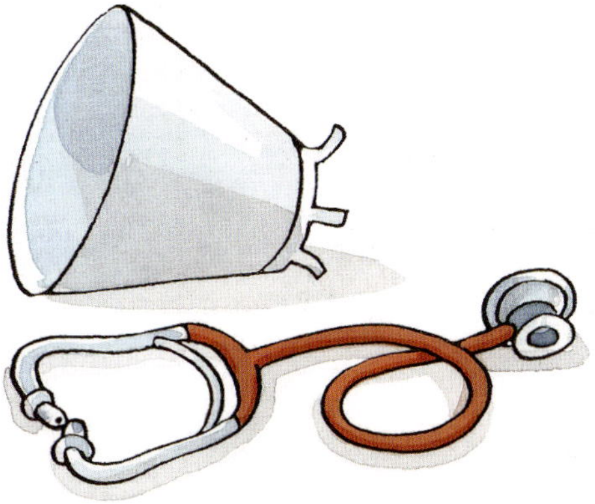

OXFORD
UNIVERSITY PRESS

Floppy chased a rabbit. The rabbit ran under a fence. Floppy went under the fence too, but he got stuck.

Dad ran to help Floppy. “Oh no!” he said. “I think Floppy has cut himself.”

Dad looked at the cut. "Sorry, Floppy," he said. "It's a deep cut. We must take you to the vet."

The children were upset. They all wanted to go to the vet with Floppy. "Poor Floppy," said Kipper.

They went to the vet. Some people were waiting. "That dog needs to see the vet first," said a man.

“Yes,” said a lady. “Let him go first. My snake can wait.”

The vet cleaned Floppy's cut. "It will need stitches," she said.

Kipper was worried. "Will it hurt him?" he asked.

“No,” said the vet. “He won’t feel anything. We’ll check him over and then we’ll help him go to sleep.”

“Will he be all right?” asked Biff.

"He'll be fine," said the vet. "Give him a big hug, then you can go home. When he wakes up, you can come and get him."

The children gave Floppy a hug.

“Poor old Floppy,” said Chip.

Floppy had the stitches and he soon woke up.
The children came with Dad to take him home.

Floppy tried to chew his stitches.

"We can't let him do that," said the vet.

The vet put a cone collar on Floppy. "He mustn't chew the stitches," she said. "This will stop him from chewing."

“Poor Floppy!” said Kipper. “The collar looks like a lampshade.”

They took Floppy home, but he didn't like the cone collar.

CRASH! He knocked over the plants. BUMP! He ran into doorways. THUMP! He knocked into the children's legs.

Kipper had an idea. “Let’s put this on him instead,” he said.

They put Kipper's old top on Floppy. He still couldn't chew his stitches, but he didn't seem to mind.

Floppy liked Kipper's top.

"It's better than a cone collar," said Kipper.

Floppy's cut was soon better. He went back to the vet to have his stitches out.

The vet checked Floppy's cut. "It's healed very well," she said.

She let Kipper listen to Floppy's heart. "He's fine," she said. "Floppy is very fit."

"He's as good as new," said the vet.
"But my old top isn't!" said Kipper.

Talk about the story

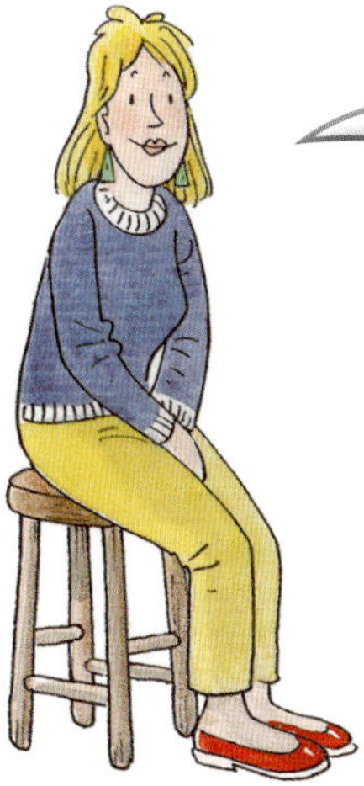

Why were the children worried when Floppy cut himself?

Why did Floppy have to have stitches?

How did Kipper feel at the end of the story?

Do you have a pet? How do you look after it?

What do you find at the vet?

Talk about the things you see on this page. Can you think of anything else you might find at the vet?

stitches

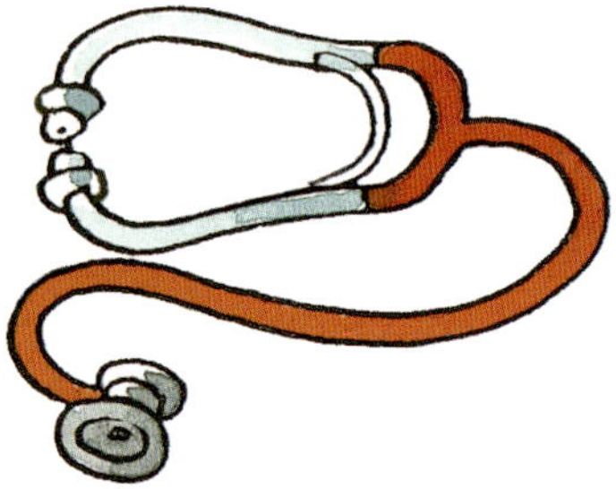

stethoscope

antiseptic

sick pet

Now look back at the story and find these things in the pictures.

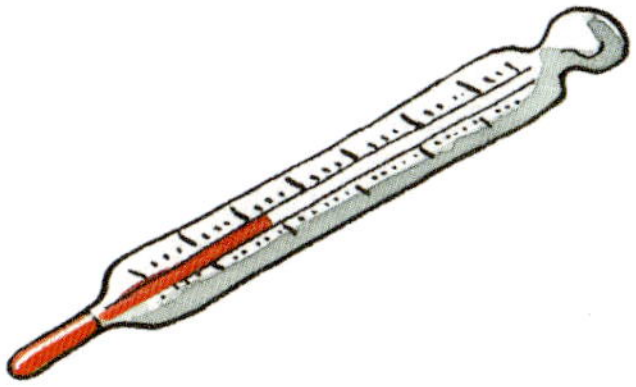

thermometer

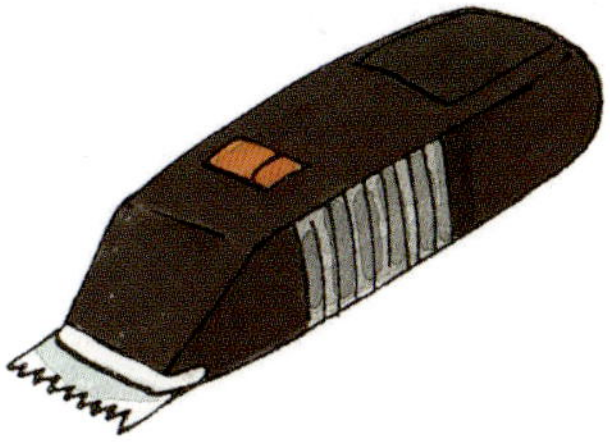

clippers

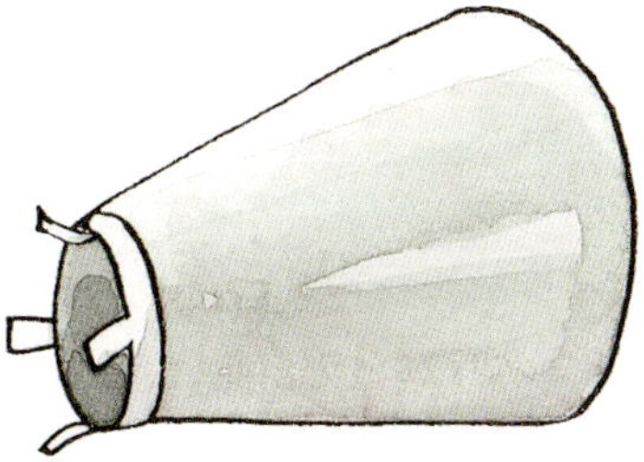

cone collar

cat box

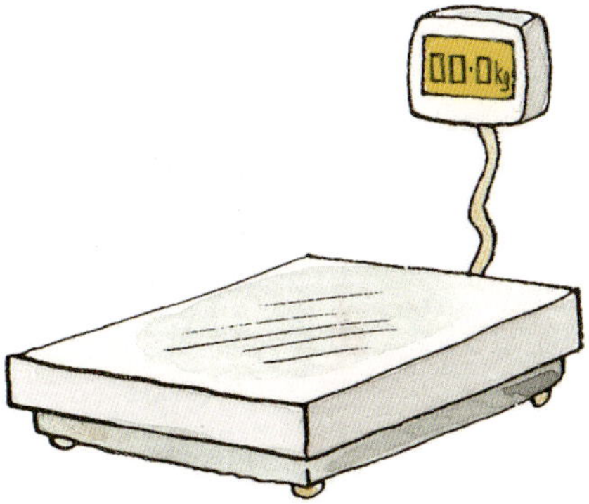

weighing scales

A Maze

Help the rabbit find its burrow.

First Experiences with Biff, Chip & Kipper
Have you read them all yet?
Kipper's First Pet
Learning to Swim
Going to the Dentist
Going to the Hairdresser
Series created by Roderick Hunt and Alex Brychta
Going to the Doctor
Going on a Plane
Let's Recycle!
Fun at the Farm
Kipper Gets Nits
Going to the Hospital
Going to the Optician
Starting School
First Experiences Flashcards
55 cards
Kipper's First Dance Class
A New Baby
Kipper's First Match
Going to the Vet
OXFORD

Read with Biff, Chip and Kipper

The UK's best-selling home reading series

	Phonics	First Stories
Level 1 Getting ready to read	Kipper's Alphabet I Spy; Chip's Letter Sounds; Biff's Wonder Words; Floppy's Fun Phonics	Get On; Floppy Did This!; Up You Go; Six in a Bed
Level 2 Starting to read	I am Kipper; Cat in a Bag; The Red Hen; The Fizz-Buzz	Funny Fish; Silly Races!; The Snowman; Dad's Birthday
Level 3 Becoming a reader	Such a Fuss; Shops; The Sing Song; The Backpack	Poor Old Rabbit; I Can Trick a Tiger; Super Dad; Floppy and the Bone
Level 4 Developing as a reader	Wet Feet; The Moon Jet; The Red Coat; Quick! Quick!	Missing!; The Raft Race; Dragon Danger; The Spaceship
Level 5 Building confidence in reading	Egg Fried Rice; Craig Saves the Day; Seasick; Dolphin Rescue	Hungry Floppy; Husky Adventure; Trapped!; Looking after Gran
Level 6 Reading with confidence	Gran's New Blue Shoes; Ice City; Save Pudding Wood; Uncle Max	Hairy-Scary Monster; Mountain Rescue; The Lost Voice; Secret of the Sands

Phonics stories help children practise their sounds and letters, as they learn to do in school.

First Stories have been specially written to provide practice in reading everyday language.

OXFORD
UNIVERSITY PRESS

Great Clarendon Street, Oxford OX2 6DP

First published 2007
This edition published 2014

10 9 8 7 6 5 4 3 2 1
Series Editors: Kate Ruttle, Annemarie Young
British Library Cataloguing in Publication Data available
ISBN: 978-0-19-273681-9
Printed in China by Imago

With thanks to Haidee Barker MRCVS and Jonathan Horrocks MRCVS